An i view with

Michael Morpurgo

Other authors in the series:

Enid Blyton, Theresa Breslin,
Gillian Cross, Anne Fine, Jamila Gavin,
Michelle Magorian, Jenny Nimmo,
Jacqueline Wilson

Joanna Carey is an author and illustrator in
her own right. She is a former children's books
editor of *The Guardian*, and still contributes.
She is also a regular reviewer for the
Times Educational Supplement.
Joanna also interviewed Jacqueline Wilson
and Jamila Gavin for this series.

First published in Great Britain 1999 by Mammoth
This edition published 2002 by Egmont Books Ltd,
239 Kensington High Street, London W8 6SA.

Interview questions, design and typesetting © 1999
Egmont Books Ltd
Interview answers © 1999 Michael Morpurgo
Michael's Books © 1999 Joanna Carey
My Father is a Polar Bear © 1999 Michael Morpurgo

ISBN 1 4052 0054 5

Contents

Foreword

When I originally interviewed Michael Morpurgo at Nethercott in 1999, nobody could have foreseen that waiting round the corner was the trauma of the foot and mouth disease epidemic, which descended in February 2001. 'Just one month after we celebrated 25 years of Farms for City Children,' Michael tells me, 'foot and mouth disease struck North Devon and the countryside and farms were closed. For eight months no children could come to any of our three farms and the whole project came perilously close to finishing.'

Michael's book *Out of the Ashes*, based on the terrible effects of the disease on the farming community, was published shortly after, and because of its topicality was swiftly made into a TV film. 'Tragically, that book was all too easy to research,' he says. 'Animals on three neighbouring farms were culled. From my bedroom window I could see and smell those carcasses burning. It was just awful . . . *but*' – and here he smiles with relief – 'thanks to friends and benefactors we survived. And children are coming again, and it's business as usual.'

Although Michael and Clare remain the key figures at Farms for City Children, and are still heavily involved with the project, they recently decided to step back a little from the practical side of running Nethercott Farm and they have handed that job over to some younger people. So there's more time, not just for their grandchildren – they have six – but also for Michael's writing. He has written several (about 12 he thinks) more books in the last three years, and he's working on screenplay adaptations of two of his books – *The Ghost of Grania O'Malley* and *The Butterfly Lion*. He was already working on the latter when I originally interviewed him, three years ago. 'These things take a long time!' he says, but he's now putting the finishing touches to

*Michael Morpurgo (b.1943) has written over 90 books, many short stories and even two musicals. His books have won the Whitbread Award (*The Wreck of the Zanzibar*), the Smarties Book Prize (*The Butterfly Lion*) and the Circle of Gold Award (*King of the Cloud Forests*), and several have been shortlisted for the Carnegie Medal. In addition, two novels have been adapted for television and film (*My Friend Walter *and* Why the Whales Came*).*

*Michael and his wife Clare were awarded an MBE in the 1999 Queen's Birthday Honours List for services for youth, in recognition of their work for the charity *Farms for City Children.

An interview with

Michael Morpurgo

by Joanna Carey

Michael Morpurgo and his wife Clare live in Devon, just a short distance from Nethercott Farm, one of the three 'Farms for City Children' that they run. They've been married for 38 years and they have two sons, Sebastian and Horatio, a daughter Rosalind, and four granddaughters. It's a cold wintry morning when I arrive, and we sit in the kitchen. A dog called Bercelet – a handsome lurcher that I think I recognise from Michael Foreman's illustrations for *Arthur, High King of Britain* – is trying to get back to sleep on the floor in front of the cooker. A huge pile of post has just arrived – letters and parcels from publishers, letters from young readers, thank-you cards from children who've been staying on the farm, invitations to literary events . . .

and a squashy parcel from an overseas fan containing a splendid pair of hand-knitted red socks for the author. He absent-mindedly pulls them on top of those he's already wearing as he tells me about his work, and how it was he came to be a writer.

* * *

Fact or fiction?

When did you start to write?

I began to write when I was a teacher, inspired by the wonderfully fresh, spontaneous, positive way the children reacted to the books I read to them in class. It made *me* read a lot more, and gradually I started to write my own stories.

I don't just write for children – and I suppose it's what a lot of authors say – but I write for the 'child in me', 'the inner child', that I suppose I still partly am. But it's rewarding to write for children – they are so much more capable of suspending their disbelief. That's not to say they lose their critical faculties, but because they themselves have such a heightened imaginative existence, they are more prepared to lose themselves in someone else's, providing of course that the story you offer them is tightly woven and convincing.

Where do the stories come from?

All over the place. Although I'm a writer of fiction, it's never a matter of pure invention. There's always a nugget of truth at the centre of each of my stories: incidents in my own life, people I've met, items remembered from TV documentaries, articles snipped out of newspapers. Anything that catches my eye, I'll hang on to it. I've got my antennae out all the time.

Certainly there's more than just a nugget of truth in one story Michael wrote recently ('My Father is a Polar Bear' in The Family Tree) – about a boy who, never having met his natural father, sees him for the first time on television.

That episode's largely autobiographical, isn't it?

Yes. I was brought up with a stepfather and I knew almost nothing about my real father when I was a child, though I had a feeling that, like my mother, he was an actor. Television was still something of a novelty at that time – we'd bought one specially to watch Princess Margaret's wedding. And in those days there was still an air of formality surrounding the watching of a programme on television. It was an event – the curtains would be closed, people would concentrate, and there was no wandering about getting cups of coffee, no channel surfing to see what else was on. I was in my late teens, and on this occasion I was watching the Christmas film with the family – my brother, my stepbrother and sister, my mother, and my stepfather and some cousins. It was a Canadian production of *Great Expectations* and we'd just got to the terrifying scene where Pip is in the graveyard, and the escaped convict, the hideous Magwitch, looms up from behind the tombstone. My cousins were screaming with fear, then, 'Oh my God!' said my mother, pointing at the screen, 'That is your father!'

What had happened, as Michael was to find out later, was that when he and his brother were very small, their parents (who were indeed both actors who had met in rep at the Marlowe Theatre in Canterbury) had been separated by the war.

Tell me about your father.

My father (the actor Tony Valentine Bridge) had gone off to fight. He was in Baghdad with the Pioneer Corps when I was born and while he was away, my mother, my brother and I were evacuated from London to escape the bombs. Then my mother fell in love with another man whom she subsequently married. The whole business was very discreetly handled. My mother never spoke about my real father, who, after failing to win her back, had gone off to live and work abroad (in Canada). I think my mother was ashamed about the divorce, as people *were* in those days, and she and my stepfather – of whom I was genuinely fond – simply preferred to bring us up as a normal happy family as if nothing had happened. So it wasn't until I was in my twenties that I actually got to meet and make friends with my real father. And at last I feel, in writing that fictionalised version of the story, that I have somehow resolved the situation.

*   *   *

My childhood

Tell me about your childhood.

I was born in 1943 in St Albans, but my first memories of family are in Philbeach Gardens in Earl's Court in London. I went to the local primary school, St Matthias. It was a church school and for some reason we shared the premises with some Greek Orthodox monks. I remember those black-clad figures flitting around the place, and I also recall that it was around this time that I had my first trip to hospital. During a game in the playground I crashed into a girl called Belinda who wore glasses, and I got glass embedded in my eyebrow.

This was the period just after the war, and our school playground was right next to a bomb site, which was interesting . . . and in a neighbouring street I remember watching some men fighting. It was the first time I'd ever seen adults being violent with one another. We then moved to Bradwell-on-Sea in Essex, and shortly after this I was sent off to join my brother at boarding school – a prep school called The Abbey, in Forest Row in Sussex. My stepfather, who was in the literary world, was very ambitious for us and had high hopes of academic success, but although I did once write something in the school magazine I never dreamed of being a writer – that was something I thought only 'really clever' people did.

I showed no particular academic talent, getting by because I was very good at sports – cricket and rugby.

Were you happy at this school?

Like the children in my books, *The War of Jenkins' Ear* and *The Butterfly Lion*, I suffered terrible pangs of homesickness, being sent away from home. I was also terrified of the dark. It was a very intense period. There was a fence round the school and we were well aware of the rift between us, in our privileged middle-class school, and the other children in the neighbourhood. We used to meet them when we went out on cross-country runs and we had regular confrontations, like the boys in *The War of Jenkins' Ear*. It was very much a 'them and us' situation.

In the closed-in community of the boarding school situation, even if you were a shy kind of person, it really didn't pay to be solitary. There was no privacy

Michael (front left) in his prep school rugby team in 1954.

whatever, except in your thoughts, so friends were desperately important. I remember it mainly as a time of music, prayer and detention. The teachers had a system of 'form orders' and if you did badly, i.e. if you got more minuses than pluses, you had to report to the headmaster who would cane you. And at night, in the dormitories, anyone who was caught out of bed would instantly be hauled off to get caned. I can still remember the sound echoing down the corridor of boys being beaten: 'Ow! Sir . . . Ow! Sir . . . Ow! Sir . . . Ow! Sir . . . Ow! Sir . . .' I'll never forget that.

I simply tried to keep out of trouble and to capitalise on things I was good at, like being in teams, winning cups, and this had the added advantage of pleasing my parents.

What were your happiest memories of the time?

Not surprisingly, my happiest memories of this period of my life are those of coming home for the holidays. We'd catch the milk train and be home in time for breakfast.

And the worst memories?

Being found out. I stole a pen from another boy and hid it in my tuck box. It was a beautiful fountain pen – I really wanted it – a Parker 'Silver Arrow'. I knew I'd transgressed. I hid it in my tuck box, but I was found out and the whole affair was made public. It really was dreadful.

What were you reading?

I used to read quite a lot at this time. My parents had always read to me when I was little – *The Wind in the Willows* is the first book I remember clearly – and the books I read at prep school were things like G.A. Henty, Robert Louis Stevenson (*Treasure Island* is still my all-time favourite book), Enid Blyton (though she was severely disapproved of) and C.S. Forester. And I did love poetry – particularly 'out loud' rather than on the page. Even as a very young child, my mother told me, I loved to play with words. At the age of three she found me rocking my bed and inexplicably chanting 'Zanzibar! Zanzibar! Marzipan! Zanzibar!'

What was the teaching like at prep school?

Although I 'got by', the lazy teaching philosophy at my prep school was intellectually limiting. It was, quite literally, the carrot and stick system, and if you didn't take the carrot they really *did* beat you with a stick!

*   *   *

Secondary school

What was your secondary school like?

At 13 I took a scholarship for King's School, Canterbury. I remember being driven down there in a Humber Super Snipe. I wasn't particularly brainy, but I got a scholarship for being what I suppose you could describe as 'a jolly good all-round sort of chap'.

Michael's last day at King's School, Canterbury, with HM the Queen Mother.

King's was a marvellous school. A wonderful headmaster, Fred Shirley – he was a bit of a dictator, but at the same time he was an inspirational character. He made you feel you really were *someone*. Things really hummed. There was a lot of music – we sang in Canterbury Cathedral and the school had a wonderful orchestra. On Sunday mornings I'd sit writing letters home to the sound of Tchaikovsky, Rachmaninov and

Beethoven. It left me with an abiding love of music –
still the source of my deepest contentment – and now I
listen to Bach and Mozart most of the time, and
Beethoven when I'm feeling solemn. And of course I
still like Buddy Holly and Elvis, and The Beatles, and I
increasingly enjoy going to the opera.

What was your favourite lesson?

My favourite lesson was French, simply because I could
do it. I had an excellent teacher and some good
exchange visits. The ability to speak French is
something I value enormously, especially now I have a
French daughter-in-law and four bilingual
grandchildren, and, of course, I can go into French
schools and talk about my books. I've been doing that
most recently with my book *Joan of Arc*. I think it's a
shame there isn't more opportunity for children here to
read books from other countries – books that reflect the
lives and experiences of their contemporaries all over
the world. There is so much being written, yet there are
so few books in translation.

Michael (far right) in the King's School, Canterbury, rugby team in 1962.

What were you reading at this stage?

I really didn't read enough at school. Perversely, I think I was psychologically put off great literature by the very fact that my parents were so enthusiastic about it (my stepfather ran the National Book League), and I think it was to escape from the academic world that my brother left school at 16 to work in the theatre. I did very little reading outside the syllabus. I hated Shakespeare, Chaucer and Jane Austen, though I loved *Tom Jones* for its fast rollicking style, and I particularly loved *Sir Gawain and the Green Knight* – oh, and the *Rime of the Ancient Mariner*.

But for pleasure I read biographies of people like

Napoleon, great generals, and the heroic, selfless exploits of explorers like Shackleton or Thor Heyerdahl.

Though it was in no way the fault of the school, intellectually, I'm ashamed to say, I completely wasted my time there. I went for the easy option – sports, games, I was in the rugby XV, the cricket XI, I was CSM of the Cadet Corps, and captain of school (which meant I got to wear a purple gown).

*   *   *

My career

What did you do when you left school?

It was agreed that I was cut out for the army, and at 18 I won a scholarship to Sandhurst Military Academy where I got the shock of my life – hair brutally shorn off, dressed in fatigues, thrust into infantry training – I grew up ten years in six months! It was a tough, humiliating experience – calculated to strip us of all the arrogance, all the airs and graces we'd accumulated at public school. I remember one

Sergeant-Major from the Coldstream Guards bellowing at me when I was late on parade: 'Mr Morpurgo, sir! If you are late on parade again I shall castrate you with the rough end of a ragman's trumpet!' No, I don't know what he meant, but you get the idea. And then there was the Duke of Kent. I've never forgiven him! He was the Senior Under Officer who gated me for having holes in my shoes! We really were put through the mill . . . reduced to simply obeying orders . . . pared down to the bone in order to be rebuilt as officers. And I found myself profoundly unwilling to be one. I realised that I'd gone right through my education without thinking about what I wanted to do, but knew now that I certainly didn't want to spend the rest of my life in the army.

There was an added dimension to all this –
Michael was in love . . .

So you left the army?

For a long time I'd been courting Clare, a girl I'd met on holiday in Corfu. We decided to marry. But that was simply not allowed: you could *not* be married *and* be at Sandhurst. So my mother cunningly sent me a telegram saying, 'MOTHER DANGEROUSLY ILL. COME IMMEDIATELY.' I was given compassionate leave and Clare and I were married at Kensington Register Office. We had a brief honeymoon at the Compleat Angler in Marlow, and the following day I took, and failed, my driving test in nearby Caversham. Clare then returned to her A level studies and I went back to Sandhurst to confess about my marriage. And I was out within 24 hours. It was like being kicked out of a nunnery.

What was your first job?

At 19, married, with a baby on the way, I found a job as a teacher in a boys' prep school in Sussex. But I soon realised I needed proper qualifications and took a degree at King's College, London, in French, English and philosophy. I then did a teaching course, and got another job in a prep school. I was reading a lot more now, and thinking properly. Gradually I became a teacher with something to teach.

It was at this time that I discovered Ted Hughes's book *Poetry in the Making* – marvellous! It really was a

Michael as a teacher
in 1970.

formative, inspirational book. But my attempts to get the children to express themselves as individuals weren't welcomed, particularly not by the head of the last independent school I taught at. He was deeply suspicious of 'creative writing', which he regarded as dangerously conspiratorial and revolutionary! (This was the school that features in *The War of Jenkins' Ear* – where the head actually did have an elephant's foot stool in the study, a school where the staff operated on the same assumptions that had prevailed 20 years before, with teachers still inculcating the notion that poorer children were a cut below.) I left this school after a serious row, when I made a formal complaint about the head's mistreatment of the boys, i.e. beating them. I was dismissed but reinstated by the union, whereupon I resigned and took a job in a state primary school in Kent.

By now the Morpurgos' second son had been born, and Clare was teaching too.

You eventually left the education system all together, didn't you?

Clare and I now had a pretty good understanding of what was involved in educating children, and a clear idea of what we wanted to achieve. We began to realise that the good *we* could do in schools was limited. We decided to explore why so many children seem to fail at school. It was increasingly clear that, metaphorically, however good the seed, if you cast it on stony ground, it won't grow.

Then, when Clare's father died (her father was Sir Allen Lane, who founded Penguin books – the man who made good books available to everyone) she received an inheritance, and we realised that we had both the means and the opportunity to 'enrich' the soil for some of these children, and to provide them with some positive experiences.

After a lot of research, we came up with the idea of setting up a farm in the country where children from deprived inner-city schools would come and stay – not just for enjoyment, but actually to work and to take an active part in the running of the farm, where they would feel needed.

So we came down to Devon, a part of the world Clare knew well from holidays with her father, and found Nethercott Farm, which, with the invaluable cooperation of the neighbouring farmers, was to become the first of the 'Farms for City Children' (FFCC). There are three farms now – in Devon, Wales and Gloucestershire.

How has this vision turned into reality?

It was a huge undertaking. Before the schools started coming we spent a year working on the farm – just finding our feet as farmers, getting to understand how it all worked – and it was in 1978 that the first school arrived (from Birmingham) to spend a week on the farm, feeding the chickens, looking after animals, sweeping, cleaning, mucking out, picking vegetables, hedging, painting – everything! And, importantly, working alongside *real* farmers. We were amazed by the physical energy of the children. We had never realised quite how much they'd be capable of, providing they were well fed, or how they would cope with often appalling weather. But again, there's no problem if they are properly clothed.

Many of the children who come have known nothing but bleak inner-city environments, have never seen a cow or a field, and are astonished by their first experience of the countryside. It's wonderful talking to the children. I think I see a side of them that neither their parents nor their teachers see. I'm always fascinated by their reactions and their comments and the imaginative, perceptive, eccentric things they say. One thing that always amazes them is the darkness. It's usually evening when they arrive down here, and they experience for the first time the pitch blackness of the countryside. And only yesterday I was talking to a ten-year-old who couldn't get over the fact that, walking round the farm, he could 'actually feel the stones in the earth' through the soles of his wellies. He'd only ever walked on asphalt and concrete before.

And when they first see the animals! They can't believe the size of them! The cute pictures of pigs they may have seen, in books for example, in no way prepare them for the enormous creatures they encounter here, rearing up over the side of the pigsty. And they see the messy side of life on the farm. They see animals being born, and they learn about death too. Quite often lambs are born dead, and that's not something they expect.

*   *   *

My career as a writer

Were you writing at this point?
I'd already had a few books published by this time. I'd had some invaluable encouragement from Aidan Chambers at Macmillan Education, and when the farm venture got going I found I could combine writing and farming, and in 1982 my book *War Horse* was published.

What caused you to write 'War Horse'?
What compelled me initially to write that was reading the war poets. I did a colossal amount of research, both in the Imperial War Museum in London and here locally, talking to people in the village who could

remember World War I. It was tremendously exciting, like detective work in a way. I learned a lot with that book, and how important it is to read massively, even if it's not all absolutely relevant. It was with *War Horse* that I found my voice as a writer, and the confidence to see writing as my profession. *War Horse* was shortlisted for the Whitbread Award that year. I remember at the ceremony Roald Dahl calling me over to talk. 'Children really don't like history you know!' he told me. But other people were a bit more encouraging.

Ted Hughes was a neighbour and a very good friend. We first met him in 1976. He came up from the river one day where he'd been fishing – he just emerged out of the mist. He not only gave us tremendous support for the farm, he wanted to be part of it. He became president of FFCC, and he also gave me a lot of encouragement as a writer. Early on he made me see the importance of recording everything that happens on the farm, 'catching moments', recording daily and capturing the rhythm of the year through the natural cycle of events. We collaborated on *All Around the Year*.

Michael with Clare (front) and Ted and Carol Hughes,
and the boy who modelled for the cover of 'Sam's Duck.'

What was Ted Hughes like to work with?

He was a great person to work with, very
straightforward, and he never let people be in awe of
him. He always read everything I wrote. If he liked it he
would respond to it, and was always very constructive
in his comments. It was he who taught me how to deal
with – i.e. disregard – criticism that is entirely negative.

Have you ever had bad reviews?

Yes, I have! Curiously, a bad review can make me feel
extra protective towards a book, and for that reason I
feel particularly fond of my book *Twist of Gold* which was

well and truly hammered by one critic.

With three children of their own (Horatio, Sebastian and Ros, whom they adopted as a baby in 1969), and with 30 or 40 children arriving on the farm each week, it's difficult to imagine exactly how Michael has found the time and the energy to write so much.

Wasn't it exhausting?

Yes it was, and often still is! Apart from all the arrivals and departures of the school, there are endless decisions to make on the farm and problems you can't anticipate, like blocked drains, sick animals, vets, fire alarms, floods . . . But whatever happens I make a point of reading once a week to the children who are staying. I often read to them from whatever it is I'm currently writing. And I'm there every evening for milking. But Clare and I do get away in the summer, in the school holidays. We go every year to the Isles of Scilly where we rent a cottage. We do a lot of walking and sailing. We first went there because one of my sons was a keen bird-watcher, and that's where I first saw the gigs – like the one Laura rowed in

The Wreck of the Zanzibar.

Islands – as lots of writers have discovered – make perfect settings for the telling of stories. *Treasure Island* is still my favourite book – and three of my books are set on the Scilly Isles.

How do you actually set about writing?

I do most of my writing in bed – well, on the bed really. I go upstairs after breakfast and sit on the bed – warm socks, lots of pillows, and the book propped up on my knees. I got the idea from a picture I once saw of R.L. Stevenson at work. Sitting at a desk gives me backache. Yes, I do get blobs of ink on the sheets, and footprints, and dog hairs. Bercelet often joins me, though she's not meant to. I write very small, with a very fine pen on lined paper in a school exercise book – no paragraphs, getting as much as I can on to one page – simply because I hate turning over and being confronted with a blank space. In fact that's one of the things I really do hate about writing – I hate starting anything. And I hate correcting things. And rewriting.

What do you like best?

What I like best is what I call the 'dream time' – thinking about a story, weaving it in my head – all the time while I'm doing other things like working on the farm, walking, driving, and of course when I'm on holiday.

How does a story develop?

Creating a story is an organic process. It's like an embryo inside an egg. If it's fertile and I'm careful to keep it warm by thinking about it, then other ideas come in, and gradually the whole thing starts taking shape. The plot becomes the bone structure, which is then fleshed out by the characters as they appear and start to interact with one another. Having hatched the idea, I find it's vitally important not to start

writing until I'm ready, or there's a danger that the story might be stillborn. But once I've started, I write very quickly – something I got used to when I didn't have so much time, when there was such a

Clare and Bercelet at home.

lot to be done on the farm and we didn't have much help. Clare always reads my manuscripts first – I respect her judgment.

What gives you most satisfaction about being a writer?

I think it's that moment when a book is newly published. It was wonderful the first time and it continues to be wonderful. I love all the letters I get, and the wonderful remarks children make, like, 'I get loads of books from the library but yours was my first "bought" book', or 'I've got two favourite authors. You're the first, then Jane Austen . . .'

It's tempting to suppose that TV, videos, CD ROMs and other forms of technology pose a threat to books and the habit of reading. Do books have a future in the twenty-first century?

Certainly technology offers all sorts of alternative forms of communication, especially TV. But it can never, never be a substitute for books. TV can offer a lot more clues in the telling of a story, but it's at its best when it's not too obvious. So often the images on TV lead you on too much, give too much away. Books are more interactive than any other medium because, through this strange code of squiggles, you can actually engage in someone else's dream. You get an interweaving of interpretations and it's up to *you* to make it work. A book is different for each person who reads it.

Do you watch much TV?

Yes, in spite of what I've just said, I do watch far too much television! *Newsnight*, chat shows, arts programmes, *Have I Got News for You*, almost everything. And I love the cinema. My favourite film stars of all time would be James Stewart and Catherine Deneuve. And it's great seeing my own books made into films (*My Friend Walter*, *When the Whales Came*) and fascinating to see the ways in which the story can be enriched in the process.

Do you get to write the screenplays?

Yes, I love to be involved in that way. I'm currently

working on *The Butterfly Lion*. It gives you a 'second bite at the cherry'. When I was writing the treatment for *The Wreck of the Zanzibar*, for example, I was able to enlarge on the character of Billy in a way that wasn't necessary or appropriate in the book. And yes, writing is a lonely profession, so it's good to have the opportunity, as on a film, to work in a team with other people.

How important to you is the visual aspect of the book?

Tremendously important. I like to be involved from the beginning if possible, and I love to be in a position where I can actually choose the illustrator, though of course that's not always possible. The illustrators I've worked with are all very different – Victor Ambrus, Michael Foreman, Christian Birmingham, Shoo Rayner, for example, all have entirely different styles and techniques. What's best is when you get an enthusiastic publisher who understands that the book starts with the design. You have a meeting where author, illustrator and editor all get together with the designer, then you get to see the roughs, the first drafts, get an idea of what the book will look like, see exactly how the illustrator is tackling the text. If you're lucky enough to get that kind of cooperation, the whole thing really comes to life. It's a collaborative affair, like making a film really!

You've done a lot of work with the artist Michael Foreman. To what extent does his work affect your writing?

I've been lucky working with Michael Foreman. He's very inventive, and the books we've done for Pavilion – *Robin Hood*, *King Arthur*, *Joan of Arc* – have largely sprung from his ideas. *Farm Boy* arose from Michael's wanting to do a book about the way farming has changed over recent generations – the impact of the machinery involved and the way the countryside changed between the 20s and the 40s.

Which of your own books is your favourite?

I suppose *Farm Boy* is my favourite book, partly because of its connection with *War Horse* – a book that's been very kind to me over the last 18 years. I love the relationship between grandfather and grandson, perhaps because I'm a grandfather now. I love the trust built between them – the old teaching the young, the young teaching the old. I love the acceptance of the old man of his life, his reverence for his memories,

The launch of
'The Wreck of the Zanzibar'.

his lack of bitterness. I loved inventing his language, hearing all the Devon voices I've known in my head as I wrote it.

Michael's Books

An overview by Joanna Carey

I disappeared on the night before my twelfth birthday, July 28, 1988. Only now can I tell the whole extraordinary story. The true story. Kensuke made me promise that I would say nothing at all, until at least ten years had passed . . . I promised, and because of that I have had to live out a lie . . . I owe it to my family and to my friends, all of whom I have deceived for so long, to tell the truth about my long disappearance, about how I lived to come back from the dead.

THUS BEGINS Michael Morpurgo's book *Kensuke's Kingdom* (pron. Kensky) – it's a portentous opening . . . a tantalising cocktail of gravity, confession and suspense – and instantly involving. Michael is a master of the first-person narrative: when he embarks on a story he doesn't keep you waiting – he simply grips your hand and helps you on board. No danger of slipping down the gap between the story and the teller – a fact that has made him one of today's most popular children's authors, and extremely productive. With over 90 titles to his name, his works include books for newly-confident readers, picture book texts, historical/classical retellings, short stories, screenplays, anthologies, operettas, and a great diversity of novels for a wide range of readers – particularly those of 11 and upwards, whose reading skills, stamina and fields of interest are rapidly expanding.

Imaginative yet realistic

Michael is an adventurous writer, not afraid to take risks, but his down-to-earth realistic style gives even the most hesitant reader a foothold on unfamiliar or unexpected territory, across a wide range of fiction.

War Horse was written in 1982, and will, for

many children, be a first experience of reading about World War I. The story is seen from all sides – the British, the French and the German – and while it is complex, richly descriptive and often harrowing (Michael never talks down to his readers), the structure ensures that it is both accessible and involving. With powerful imagery and strong characterisation, it is beautifully paced and the persuasive realism is such that it never seems anything other than perfectly normal that the perceptive and very companionable narrator should be a horse.

And in *My Friend Walter*, a high-spirited ghost story about Sir Walter Raleigh, even the ghost has a robust reality. Far from being a flimsy phantom, he's a well-rounded sympathetic character who, with his witty dialogue, his eccentric enthusiasms and his genuine concern for his descendants, is a very believable presence as he sets about restoring their fortunes. Although he very seldom strays into the realm of fantasy, Michael's insatiable appetite for research is such that historically and, geographically, distance is no object – as witness his fine retellings (in collaboration with artist Michael Foreman) of the Arthurian legends, Robin Hood and Joan of Arc. He breathes new life into these stories with the device of a present-day framing narrative which in each case takes you, as it were, round to the back of the story and lets you in through a secret entrance – as in *Arthur, High King of Britain* which begins when a young boy is very nearly drowned at sea on a foolhardy swimming expedition. He regains consciousness in a mysterious cave watched over by an ancient bearded man, Arthur Pendragon, who for 1,400 years has been waiting for just such a messenger to arrive . . .

Children and relationships

Living in Devon, and closely involved with Farms for City Children (the charity he runs with his wife, Clare), Michael writes with an easy familiarity about the countryside, wildlife and the natural rhythms of the year. And it's clear from his books that the large number of eight- to twelve-year-olds who visit the farm gives him a unique insight into the way children think and talk. Naturally, many of these children find their way into his stories – like Jessie in *The Ghost of Grania O'Malley*. This story is set in Ireland, and Jessie is doggedly determined to overcome the physical disability that others assume will prevent her from climbing the Big Hill. And many of the books – like *Sam's Duck*, *Conker* and *Colly's Barn* – show with humour and sensitivity how children, even the most timid, can express themselves through their interaction with animals.

With stories spanning almost the whole of the twentieth century, Michael is a canny observer of family life in all its infinite variety, subtly reflecting society's ever-changing attitudes to, and expectations of, children. He explores with insight the hopes, fears and uncertainties that children experience: issues of responsibility, freedom, self-esteem, and the choices they have to make if they are to have any say in their own destiny. Adults are never marginalised, women have strong roles, parents are always well drawn, but are often preoccupied (and frequently absent) and some of the strongest, most memorable relationships he creates are those between young and old. There's Laura and her grandmother in *The Wreck of the Zanzibar*; there's the young lad and his grandfather in *Farm Boy*; Gracie and Daniel, who befriend the eccentric Birdman, in *Why the Whales Came*; and Cessie, who helps her old grandad Popsicle, in *Escape from Shangri-La*, to come to terms with his confused and terrifying memories of Dunkirk in World War II. And, of course, there's the unforgettable old lady who befriends the runaway schoolboy in *The Butterfly Lion* – a beautifully structured book which, with its powerful symbolism and its underlying theme of loyalty, manages to be a love story, an animal story, a war story, and even a ghost story, all rolled into one and which, like many of his books, appeals across a wide age range – a book that really can be shared by children and parents alike.

Children in Michael's books seldom hunt in packs, and with the first-person narrative he so often favours – he writes with ease from both a male and a female point of view – he frequently offers the reader an intimate understanding of the protagonist as friend and confidant.

Time and place

Wherever Michael's stories take you, there is always a powerful 'sense of place' – whether it's the Isles of Scilly, which provide the background for several of his books, the mountains of Tibet (*King of the Cloud Forests*), the French Pyrenees (*The Dancing Bear*), the African Veld (*The Butterfly Lion*), the battlefields of World War I (*War Horse*), or the playing fields of the boarding school in his unnerving school story, *The War of Jenkins' Ear*.

The Wreck of the Zanzibar is set in the Isles of Scilly in 1907. Islands hold a particular fascination for Michael, and the small scale of the island of Bryher makes it a perfect microcosmic arena for this unusual and beautifully crafted novel, which tells the story of a small rural community fighting for survival in the face of grinding poverty, harsh weather and high seas. Apart from an introductory narrative that serves to get the reader safely across the gangplank – and back to the beginning of the century – this whole story is told in extracts from 14-year-old Laura's diary for the year 1907. Laura, in the privacy of her journal, expresses herself with an eloquent, forthright intensity, creating a vivid picture of her life, her family, her hopes, her fears, her frustrations and, in particular, her fierce resentment of the fact that as a girl she is not allowed the freedom enjoyed by her twin brother, Billy. She longs to row out to sea like Billy, but her father won't hear of it – her job is with the hens and the milking. With its gloriously atmospheric mix of elemental forces, human frailty and powerful emotion, this small but beautifully orchestrated piece – only 122 pages – takes on epic proportions as the story reaches its climax.

Why the Whales Came is also set in the Isles of Scilly. It's 1914 and, against a wartime background, with parents preoccupied with hardship and anxiety, Gracie and her friend Daniel lead a life of freedom and adventure on the island. They even get to know the eccentric 'Birdman' and, in a story rich in mystery and superstition, they unravel the truth behind his strange reclusive way of life.

Waiting for Anya is set in the French Pyrenees during World War II and, like *Friend or Foe* and *Mr Nobody's Eyes*, reflects the vastly different experiences of children whose lives are either directly or indirectly affected by war.

Michael himself grew up in the post-war period of the 50s, and he brilliantly captures the atmosphere of this period in a strangely gripping school story, *The War of Jenkins' Ear*. Inspired by the author's own experiences, and rich both in period detail and psychological intensity, it's the story of Toby, a pupil in the fortress-like close community of a private boys' prep school. Under this archaic regime the boys endure a life of corporal punishment, homesickness, bullying, fiercely competitive sports, compulsory rice pudding, fervent hero worship, and routine class warfare with local 'oiks'. Within the framework of what at first seems to be a conventional school story, Michael shows a sharper side to his pen; he not only explores matters of class, privilege, hypocrisy, loneliness – and the first stirrings of romance – but also introduces an unnerving religious element with a new boy called Simon Christopher, who claims to be Jesus Christ. Toby befriends him, and strange things begin to happen.

Isolation and 'Kensuke's Kingdom'

Making sense of the world is what, in one way or another, all good books enable children to do, and whether it's their experience of their immediate circumstances – family, friends, school – or, on a broader scale, their widening perceptions of life as it unrolls before them, there are certain themes and scenarios to which Michael returns again and again: the child away from home, separated – or estranged – from his parents, facing difficult situations, and obliged to make difficult moral, ethical and personal decisions.

His recent book, *Kensuke's Kingdom*, embraces all these but, with a radical change in his writing style, Michael has pared down his story-telling technique to bare essentials. On a much broader canvas, employing a sparse, almost skeletal prose style, he focuses on just two main characters – one of them a 12-year-old boy, away from home, separated from his parents, forced to make some difficult decisions . . .

Up until the 1950s, British authors had no trouble in isolating children for the purposes of a story: there were all the options of boarding school, quarantine, war, evacuation, parents on overseas postings, lengthy sea voyages and long stays in hospital. In these days of comprehensive schools, air travel and medical advances, there are far fewer opportunities for parent-free adventure – and neither parents nor authors would see fit to send children off alone on cycling holidays, camping out like the Famous Five any more.

But in *Kensuke's Kingdom*, the author finds an uncompromising way to wrench his young hero, Michael, away from his mum and dad. Michael is a very ordinary boy whose constant companions are his dog and his football. The story starts with his parents' redundancy and a momentous family decision to sell up and take off round the world in a yacht. Months after leaving England, disaster strikes: Michael and the dog (and the football) are lost overboard in the Pacific. Eventually they are washed up on a desert island where the only inhabitant is an elderly Japanese man, a survivor of World War II, who has been marooned there for 40 years (that's 12 years longer than Robinson Crusoe, to whom this story owes more than a little). Across the distance of history the two cultures meet – old man and young boy – the one with his roots in the past, the other with his hopes in the future. With virtually no common language the two must learn to co-exist.

It's a bold, almost preposterous story – on the scale of a fairytale really – but, narrated with an urgent economy by the boy, and haltingly by the old man as he gradually remembers a little English, it becomes frighteningly real – a gripping exploration not just of the art of survival, but also of vaster concepts like civilization, communication and hope.

An unstoppable storyteller

I once heard Michael talking about his work

at the Edinburgh Book Festival. He stepped modestly on to the platform – a serious, gentlemanly type, with a military bearing and an armful of books – but as the reading progressed, latent dramatic skills were unleashed, and with just a couple of chairs for props, and some unsuspecting volunteers from an audience of schoolchildren, we saw before us a crazed, sadistic schoolmaster, a masked executioner, a headless Elizabethan ghost, an ancient bearded sage and, above all, an inspired, passionate – and seemingly unstoppable – storyteller.

Joanna Carey

1999

Bibliography

A selection

Long Way Home

Macmillan 1975 (hb); Mammoth 1994 (pb)

George, aged 12, is in his seventh foster home, a farm owned by the Dyers. Years of rejection have made it difficult for him to make friends, but meeting Tom and his talkative sister Storme makes him face up to himself and the reality of his search for a secure home.

Friend or Foe

Macmillan 1977 (hb); Mammoth 1989 (pb)

Two young evacuees are faced with a terrible dilemma

when a German airman saves one of them from drowning, and then asks for help in return.

The Marble Crusher

Heinemann 1992 (hb); Mammoth 1994 (3-in-1 with Colly's Barn *and* Conker*)*

When Albert, a boy from the country, joins Sid Creedy's class, Sid thinks he'll have some fun. He tells Albert some outrageous stories about the teachers and Albert, a trusting lad, believes them all – until the tale of the Marble Crusher reaches the ears of the Head Teacher.

The Nine Lives of Montezuma

Kaye and Ward 1980 (hb); Mammoth 1993 (pb)

Montezuma, the farmyard cat, gradually changes through his nine lives of danger and excitement, from fiery kitten to a tired old tom-cat, always independent, a law unto himself.

The White Horse of Zennor

and other stories

Kaye and Ward 1982 (hb); Mammoth 1991 (pb)

Five haunting stories for children, including the tale of a magical horse given in return for help and how it saves a farm, and how a crippled boy learns to swim with the seals and finally goes to join them.

War Horse

Kaye and Ward 1982 (hb); Mammoth 1990 (pb)

Joey and Albert, growing up together on a West Country farm, are as close as a yearling colt and a young lad can be. But in 1914 Albert's father sells Joey to the army, in which he faces terrifying adventures and touches the lives of many people on the Western Front.

Runner-up for the Whitbread Award 1982

Twist of Gold

Kaye and Ward 1983 (hb); Mammoth 1991 (pb)

When Ireland is stricken by the potato famine, Sean and Annie, the only surviving children of the O'Brien family, set off to find their father in America. They are ill-equipped to make such a journey, possessing only a Dragoon's scarlet cloak, a shimmering moon-shawl and 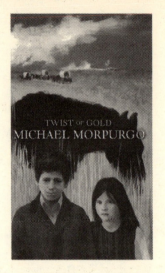 a golden necklace, but they are not prepared to give up without a fight.

Little Foxes

Kaye and Ward 1984 (hb); Mammoth 1990 (pb)

Billy Bunch, an unloved orphan, finds a den of foxes in the secret wilderness by a ruined church, and joins in their fight against the hunters.

Why the Whales Came

Heinemann 1985 (hb);

Scholastic 1985 (pb)

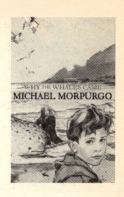

No one really believed in the curse of Samson until the whale was washed up on the beach. Will the cycle of disaster begin all over again?

Adapted for a film – When the Whales Came (1989) – by Golden Swan Films

Tom's Sausage Lion

Transworld 1979, A&C Black 1986

Tom sees a lion in his orchard, but no one believes him. So he sets out to prove it – with the help of some sausages!

Jojo, the Melon Donkey

Andre Deutsch 1987 (picture book); Heinemann 1995 (hb); Mammoth 1999 (pb)

The Doge of Venice wants to buy his daughter a beautiful horse for her birthday, but she prefers Jo-Jo, an ordinary donkey belonging to a melon seller.

King of the Cloud Forests

Heinemann 1987 (hb); Mammoth 1997 (pb)

A gripping survival adventure in which Ashley and Uncle Sung are on the run heading to India, but Uncle Sung is forced to abandon Ashley in the remote Tibetan mountains while he looks for food.

Circle of Gold Award; Prix Sorcière (France); shortlisted for the Carnegie Medal

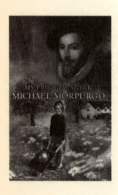

My Friend Walter

Heinemann 1988 (hb); Mammoth 1989 (pb)

Bess Throckmorton is surprised to discover that she is related to Sir Walter Raleigh. But when a ghostly stranger takes her to the Tower of London, her family's destiny changes dramatically.

Adapted for a television film by Portobello Films and WonderWorks. Shortlisted for the Smarties Prize

The Mudpuddle Farm series

(with Shoo Rayner)

A series of books featuring the characters of Mudpuddle Farm – Jigger, Mossop, Egbert the goat, Albertine the goose and Pintsize the piglet, to name just a few.

Mossop's Last Chance

A&C Black 1988; Collins 1989

Albertine, Goose Queen

A&C Black 1989; Collins 1989

Jigger's Day Off

A&C Black 1990; Collins 1990

And Pigs Might Fly!

A&C Black 1991

Martians at Mudpuddle Farm

A&C Black 1992; Collins 1993

Mum's The Word

A&C Black 1995; HarperCollins 1996

Mr Nobody's Eyes

Heinemann 1989; Mammoth 1990

Harry's life is never the same after his mother remarries,

a problem compounded by trouble
at school. When Ocky the chimp
escapes from the circus, Harry joins
his only friend in running away.

Conker

Heinemann 1987 (hb); Mammoth 1994 (pb and 3-in-1 with
The Marble Crusher *and* Colly's Barn*)*

Nick goes to collect conkers from Cotter's Yard and finds
a half-starved dog chained up. He leaves with the
conkers, but decides to rescue the dog later.

Waiting for Anya

Heinemann 1990 (hb); Mammoth 1991 (pb)

When Jo first met him, he was not to
know that the stranger's life lay in
his hands. But trust is the key to
survival in a remote Pyrennean
village during World War II, and by
honouring his promise not to
mention him to anyone, Jo becomes

drawn into the perilous network helping Jews to escape
over the border.

*Shortlisted for the Carnegie Medal and the Guardian
Fiction Award*

Colly's Barn

Heinemann 1991 (hb); Mammoth 1994 (3-in-1 with The
Marble Crusher *and* Conker); *Mammoth 1999 (pb)*
Annie's father is talking of demolishing the old barn,
but what will happen to the birds that live there? Colly
the Swallow and Screecher the Barn Owl work together
to save the barn in a remarkable way.

The Sandman and the Turtles

Heinemann 1991 (hb); Mammoth 1992 (pb)

Mike enjoys staying with his cousins on the Welsh coast, especially his grandfather's remarkable stories, although he thinks Polly is silly to believe them. But this summer is different, because they really do come  true, and the Sandman, the turtles and a Russian submarine make it a holiday to remember.

The War of Jenkins' Ear

Heinemann 1993 (hb); Mammoth 1994 (pb)

Back at boarding school, Toby Jenkins is homesick, as usual. However, things turn out to be different this term: there's Wanda, who gives Toby his first kiss; and there's new boy, Simon Christopher, with whom he forms a friendship. But this is no ordinary friendship, and Simon is no ordinary boy.

Shortlisted for the Smarties Prize 1993

US: ALA Best Book 1994

Snakes and Ladders

Heinemann 1994

Wendy doesn't know what to take for the display table on parents' evening; but then Grandad falls ill and she's left to look after his pet snake Slinky, so she pops him into her schoolbag. But when Slinky disappears, Wendy's special plan turns into a nightmare.

Ghostly Haunts

(editor), Pavilion 1994

Ten ghost stories set against the backdrop of various National Trust properties. Published to coincide with the centenary of the National Trust.

Arthur, High King of Britain

(with Michael Foreman), Pavilion 1994; Mammoth 1996

A compelling modern retelling of the legend of King Arthur and his Knights of the Round Table, told from the point of view of King Arthur himself.

Shortlisted for the Carnegie Medal

The Dancing Bear

Collins 1992

A young girl discovers a bearcub, Bruno, and looks after him. The two grow up as best friends – inseparable until the day a film crew come to the village.

Muck and Magic: Tales from the Countryside

(editor) Heinemann 1995 (hb); Mammoth 1995 (pb)

An anthology of stories written in support of the charity Farms for City Children.

The Wreck of the Zanzibar

Heinemann 1995 (hb); Mammoth 1995 (pb)

It is 1907 and life on the Scilly Isles is bleak and difficult. Winter storms give way to a wretched summer, and family after family moves to the mainland. Laura's father is driven to admit defeat, when a violent storm brings an unexpected harvest to the island.

Winner of: IBBY Honour Book of 1998; Children's Book Awards 1996 (longer novel section); Whitbread Award 1995 (children's category). Shortlisted for: Smarties Book Prize 1995; Sheffield Children's Book Award; Writer's Guild Award 1995; Carnegie Medal 1996

Blodin the Beast

Francis Lincoln 1995

A terrible beast stalks the land, enslaving the people, burning as he goes. Only Hosea can stop him, but he has to keep faith.

Sam's Duck

Collins 1996 (hb); Picture Lions 1997 (pb)

Sam is on a school trip to a farm when he rescues a duck that he sees being mistreated and smuggles it back to the city as a present for his grandad.

Screenplay, filmed by BBC TV

The King in the Forest

Simon & Schuster 1993; Hodder 2002

A young woodcutter hides a fawn, a white stag, from

the King and his hunters, helped by the young princess. Years later they fall in love, but the only way he can marry her is to bring the King the antlers of the great white stag.

The Butterfly Lion

HarperCollins 1996

A young boy rescues an orphaned white lion cub from the African bush.

Smarties Book Prize Gold Award 1996; Writer's Guild Award 1996

The Ghost of Grania O'Malley

Heinemann 1996 (hb);

Mammoth 1997 (pb)

Spirited and stubborn young Jessie O'Malley is a fighter, struggling to be accepted in spite of her 'cerebral lousy palsy', as she calls her disability. With her American cousin Jack she must fight to save the Big Hill on Clare

Island, and together they discover the joys and perils of a real adventure.

Children's Book Award 1996 for the book which was deemed to do the most to put forward a positive image of children with special educational needs (specially commended)

Robin of Sherwood

(with Michael Foreman) Harcourt Brace 1996 (US);

Hodder 1998 (pb)

The complete story of Robin Hood, from the capture of his father and Robin's subsequent befriendment by the misfits in Sherwood Forest, to his rescue of King Richard in Austria and his lapse into corruption.

Beyond the Rainbow Warrior

(editor) Pavilion 1996

Published to celebrate 25 years of campaigning by the organisation Greenpeace, a collection of tales on an ecological theme, which range from a remote New Zealand forest to the legend of the original Rainbow Warrior.

Escape from Shangri-La

Heinemann 1998 (hb); Mammoth 1999 (pb)

Cessie has never seen her grandfather until the day he turns up out of nowhere. He has a stroke and loses his memory, and Cessie's father puts him in an old people's home called 'Shangri-La'. Cessie determines to help him escape and regain his memory.

Red Eyes at Night

Hodder 1998

Millie decides to teach her show-off cousin a lesson by telling her a ghost story that ends up frightening both of them.

Cock-a-doodle-doo, Mr Sultana

Scholastic 1998

A retelling of an Old Hungarian folk tale about a cheeky

cockerel who gets his own back on the great Sultan.

Joan of Arc

(with Michael Foreman), Pavilion 1998

The story of the heroic Joan of Arc, whose vision from God led France to conquer the English, but who was later tried as a witch and burned at the stake by the humiliated English.

Farm Boy

Collins 2000 (pb)

The sequel to *War Horse*, this is a story about the relationship between a boy and his grandfather who is a farmer, and Joey the old war horse returned from World War I.

Wartman

Barrington Stoke 1998

Dilly has a wart on his knee called George, which causes him a lot of grief, both at home and at school, that is until he meets old Mr Ben.

Kensuke's Kingdom

Heinemann 1999 (hb);

Egmont 2000 (pb)

Michael is thrown overboard during a round-the-world yachting adventure with his parents. He is washed up on a remote tropical island whose sole inhabitant is a Japanese ex-soldier. Kensuke survived World War II and the bombing of Hiroshima. Content to be cut off from human contact, at first he is reluctant to share his island. Then an extraordinary bond forms between them which makes it difficult for Kensuke to let go.

Children's Book Award 2000; Prix Sorcière (France) 2001; Shortlisted for the Whitbread Award 2000

The Rainbow Bear

Doubleday 1999 (hb)

Snow bear is a king in his white wilderness, a hunter who fears no one and whose freedom is complete. But when he sees a beautiful rainbow arching over the sky he is dazzled by its colours and can think of one thing only: he wants to catch the rainbow.

Wombat Goes Walkabout

Picture Lions 1999 (hb)

Wombat digs the deepest hole he's ever dug and crawls into the cool darkness to think. But when he climbs out again, he can't see his mother anywhere. As he wanders through the great outback looking for her, Wombat meets all kinds of wonderful creatures – Kookaburra, Wallaby, Possum, Emu, Boy and Koala. None of them think very much of him, but when a fire sweeps through the bush, it is Wombat's skills that save the day.

Prix Sorcière (France) 2001

The Silver Swan

Corgi 2000 (hb)

An exquisite picture book, telling the romantic story of a family of swans on a Scottish loch and the boy who watches over them.

Dear Olly

Collins 2000 (hb)

Olly's brother Matt wants to go and work with children

who have been made orphans, through war, in Africa. He wants to be a clown and make them laugh but his mother and sister want him to stay in England and go to university.

Shortlisted for the Sheffield Book Award

Black Queen

Corgi 2000 (pb)

When Billy's mysterious next door neighbour asks him to take care of her cat while she is away, Billy cannot resist the opportunity to nose around her house. But of course, he gets more than he bargained for . . .

Billy the Kid

Collins 2000 (pb)

Billy was a champion soccer star, playing for Chelsea until the outbreak of war in 1939. His passion for football sees him through the war years, but having been injured by a mine he cannot play on his return to England and turns to vagrancy. This tale is told through the voice of an 80-year-old man, who looks back on his life as a champion striker.

From Hereabout Hill

Mammoth 2000 (pb)

A collection of Michael's short stories, reflecting his love of myths and legends, his concern that we learn from the past, his keen sense of place and his skill as a brilliant observer of family life.

Who's a Big Bully Then?

Barrington's Stoke 2001 (pb)

Beating the school bully in a race feels good, but what happens when the school bully then decides he wants a fight? Darren Bishop is about to find out what it's like to stand up for himself.

Toro! Toro!

Collins 2001 (pb)

Antonito lives an idyllic life on his parent's bull farm in Spain. But his world is shattered when he realises that his beloved bull calf, Paco, is destined for the bullring. He can't let this happen. Antonito comes up with a plan of such daring that it will take enormous courage to see it through. But it is 1936, and the drums of war echo across the Spanish plains. Little does Antonito realise the full consequences of his actions . . .

Mairi's Mermaid

Egmont 2001 Blue Banana (pb)

Mairi's brother Robbie says swimming is easy if you just pretend you're a mermaid. But that doesn't help Mairi, she been trying all summer. Besides, she isn't even sure that mermaids are real. That is, until she finds a tiny mermaid, and rescues her from a ferocious crab.

More Muck and Magic

(editor) Egmont 2001 (pb)

Illustrated by Quentin Blake.

New short stories bursting with humour, warmth

and adventure by some of the best children's writers: Joan Aiken, Gillian Cross, Jamila Gavin, Jan Mark, Margaret Mahy, Sam McBratney, Michael Morpurgo and Jacqueline Wilson; with poems by Ted Hughes.

Out of the Ashes

Macmillan 2001 (pb)

On January 1st 2001, Becky Morley begins to write her diary. By March 12th, her world has changed for ever. The foot and mouth epidemic began miles away, but now the nightmare is drawing near. Will their cattle and pigs escape the cull? And what about Josh, her hand-reared lamb? Becky's diary unfolds the fears, the guilt and the awful reality as the animals are slaughtered, in a poignant story of a community and a family in crisis.

Shortlisted for the WHSmith Award, the Children's Book Award, the Sheffield Book Award, the Portsmouth Book Award. Filmed by BBC TV 2001.

Because a Fire was in my Head

(editor) Faber 2001 (hb)

Illustrated by Quentin Blake.

A stunning collection of poems for children, from authors as diverse as Spike Milligan, Stevie Smith, Lewis Carroll and John Lennon.

The Last Wolf

Doubleday 2002 (hb)

A beautiful and lyrical tale, ranging from the highlands to the high seas, about the last wolf in Scotland.

The Sleeping Sword

Egmont 2002 (hb)

Blinded in an accident, Bun Bendle stumbles one day into an underground tomb containing a shield and a beautiful, ancient sword. As he touches the hilt, his whole body is gripped by an incredible, centuries-old power. It is a power that will change Bun's life for ever.

Short Stories

Michael has written many short stories including:

'What does it feel like?' in *In Between:*
Stories of Leaving Childhood

'Letter from Kalymnos' in *All For Love*
(Mammoth 1997)

'Mairi's Mermaid' in *Snake on the Bus and other Pet Stories*

Musicals

Solar *(music by Phylis Tate, OUP 1979)*

Scarecrow *(music by Phylis Tate, OUP 1979)*

My Father is a Polar Bear

Michael Morpurgo

This story is a tissue of truth – mostly. As with many of my stories, I have woven truths together and made from them a truth stranger than fiction. My father was a polar bear – honestly.

Tracking down a polar bear shouldn't be that difficult. You just follow the pawprints – easy enough for any competent Innuit. My father is a polar bear. Now if you had a father who was a polar bear, you'd be curious, wouldn't you? You'd go looking for him. That's what I did, I went looking for him, and I'm telling you he wasn't at all easy to find.

In a way I was lucky, because I always had two

fathers. I had a father who *was* there – I called him Douglas – and one who wasn't there, the one I'd never even met – the polar bear one. Yet in a way he was there. All the time I was growing up he was there inside my head. But he wasn't only in my head, he was at the bottom of our Start-Rite shoebox, our secret treasure box, with the rubber bands round it, which I kept hidden at the bottom of the cupboard in our bedroom. So how, you might ask, does a polar bear fit into a shoebox? I'll tell you.

My big brother Terry first showed me the magazine under the bedclothes, by torchlight, in 1948 when I was five years old. The magazine was called *Theatre World*. I couldn't read it at the time, but he could. (He was two years older than me, and already mad about acting and the theatre and all that – he still is.) He had saved up all his pocket money to buy it. I thought he was crazy. 'A shilling! You can get about a hundred lemon sherbets for that down at the shop,' I told him.

Terry just ignored me and turned to page twenty-seven. He read it out: 'The Snow Queen, a dramat – something or other – of Hans Andersen's famous story, by the Young Vic Company.' And there was a large black and white photograph right across the page – a photograph of two fierce looking polar bears bearing their teeth and about to eat two children, a boy and a girl, who looked very frightened.

'Look at the polar bears,' said Terry. 'You see that one on the left, the fatter one? That's our dad, our real dad. It says his name and everything – Peter Van Diemen. But you're not to tell. Not Douglas, not even Mum, promise?'

'My dad's a polar bear?' I said. As you can imagine I was a little confused.

'Promise you won't tell,' he went on, 'or I'll give you a Chinese burn.'

Of course I wasn't going to tell, Chinese burn or no Chinese burn. I was hardly going to go to school the next day and tell everyone that I had a polar bear for a father, was I? And I certainly couldn't tell my mother, because I knew she never liked it if I ever asked about my real father. She always insisted that Douglas was the only father I had. I knew he wasn't, not really. So did she, so did Terry, so did Douglas. But for some reason that was always a complete mystery to me, everyone in the house pretended that he was.

Some background might be useful here. I was born, I later found out, when my father was a soldier in Baghdad during the Second World War. (You didn't know there were polar bears in Baghdad, did you?) Sometime after that my mother met and fell in love with a dashing young officer in the Royal Marines called Douglas Macleish. All this time, evacuated to the Lake District away from the bombs, blissfully unaware of the war and Douglas, I was learning to walk and talk and do my business in the right place at the right time.

So my father came home from the war to discover that his place in my mother's heart had been taken. He did all he could to win her back. He took her away on a week's cycling holiday in Suffolk to see if he could rekindle the light of their love. But it was hopeless. By the end of the week they had come to an amicable arrangement. My father would simply disappear, because he didn't want to 'get in the way'. They would get divorced quickly and quietly, so that Terry and I could be brought up as a new family with Douglas as our father. Douglas would adopt us and give us Macleish as our surname. All my father insisted upon was that Terry and I should keep Van Diemen as our middle name. That's what happened. They divorced. My father disappeared, and at the age of three I became Andrew Van Diemen Macleish. It was a mouthful then and it's a mouthful now.

So Terry and I had no actual memories of our father whatsoever. I do have vague recollections of standing on a railway bridge somewhere near Earl's Court in London, where we lived, with Douglas' sister – Aunt Betty, as I came to know her – telling us that we had a brand new father who'd be looking after us from now on. I was really not that concerned, not at the time. I was much more interested in the train that was chuffing along under the bridge, wreathing us in a fog of smoke.

My first father, my real father, my missing father, became a taboo person, a big hush hush taboo person that no one ever mentioned, except for Terry and me. For us he soon became a sort of secret phantom father. We used to whisper about him under the blankets at night. Terry would sometimes go snooping in my mother's desk and he'd find things out about him. 'He's an actor,' Terry told me one night. 'Our dad's an actor, just like Mum is, just like I'm going to be.'

It was only a couple of weeks later that he brought the

theatre magazine home. After that we'd take it out again and look at our polar bear father. It took some time, I remember, before the truth of it dawned on me – I don't think Terry can have explained it very well. If he had, I'd have understood it much sooner – I'm sure I would. The truth, of course – as I think you might have guessed by now – was that my father was both an actor *and* a polar bear at one and the same time.

Douglas went out to work a lot and when he was home he was a bit silent, so we didn't really get to know him. But we did get to know Aunty Betty. Aunty Betty simply adored us, and she loved giving us treats. She wanted to take us on a special Christmas treat, she said. Would we like to go to the zoo? Would we like to go to the pantomime? There was *Dick Whittington* or *Puss in Boots*. We could choose whatever we liked.

Quick as a flash, Terry said, '*The Snow Queen*. We want to go to *The Snow Queen*.'

So there we were a few days later, Christmas Eve 1948, sitting in the stalls at a matinee performance of *The Snow Queen* at the Young Vic theatre, waiting, waiting for the moment when the polar bears come on. We didn't have to wait for long. Terry nudged me and pointed, but I knew already which polar bear my father had to be. He was the best one, the snarliest one, the growliest one, the scariest one. Whenever he came on he really looked as if he was going to eat someone, anyone. He looked mean and hungry and savage, just the way a polar bear should look.

I have no idea whatsoever what happened in *The Snow Queen*. I just could not take my eyes off my polar bear father's curling claws, his slavering tongue, his killer eyes. My father was without doubt the finest polar bear actor the world had ever seen. When the great red curtains closed at the end and opened again for the actors to take their bows, I clapped so hard that my hands hurt. Three more curtain calls and the curtains stayed closed. The safety curtain came down and my father was cut off from me, gone, gone for ever. I'd never see him again.

Terry had other ideas. Everyone was getting up, but Terry stayed sitting. He was staring at the safety curtain as if in some kind of trance. 'I want to meet the polar bears,' he said quietly.

Aunty Betty laughed. 'They're not bears, dear, they're actors, just actors, people acting. And you can't meet them, it's not allowed.'

'I want to meet the polar bears,' Terry repeated. So did I, of course, so I joined in. 'Please, Aunty Betty,' I pleaded. 'Please.'

'Don't be silly. You two, you do get some silly notions sometimes. Have a Choc Ice instead. Get your coats on now.' So we each got a Choc Ice. But that wasn't the end of it.

We were in the foyer caught in the crush of the crowd when Aunty Betty suddenly noticed that Terry was missing. She went loopy. Aunty Betty always wore a fox stole, heads still attached, round her shoulders. Those poor old foxes looked every bit as pop-eyed and frantic as she did, as she plunged through the crowd, dragging me along behind her and calling for Terry.

Gradually the theatre emptied. Still no Terry. There was quite a to-do, I can tell you. Policemen were called in off the street. All the programme sellers joined in the search, everyone did. Of course, I'd worked it out. I knew exactly where Terry had gone, and what he was up to. By now Aunty Betty was sitting down in the foyer and sobbing her heart out. Then, cool as a cucumber, Terry appeared from nowhere, just wandered into the foyer.

Aunty Betty crushed him to her, in a great hug. Then she went loopy all over again, telling him what a naughty, naughty boy he was, going off like that. 'Where were you? Where have you been?' she cried.

'Yes, young man,' said one of the policemen. 'That's something we'd all like to know as well.'

I remember to this day exactly what Terry said, the very words: 'Jimmy riddle. I just went for a jimmy riddle.' For just a moment he even had me believing him. What an actor! Brilliant.

We were on the bus home, right at the front on the top deck where you can guide the bus round corners all by yourself – all you have to do is steer hard on the white bar in front of you. Aunty Betty was sitting a couple of rows behind us. Terry made quite sure she wasn't looking. Then, very surreptiously, he took something out from under his coat and showed me. The programme. Signed right across it were these words, which Terry read out to me:

> 'To Terry and Andrew,
> With love from your polar bear father, Peter.
> Keep happy.'

Night after night I asked Terry about him, and night after night under the blankets he'd tell me the story again, about how he'd gone into the dressing-room and found our father sitting there in his polar bear costume with his head off (if you know what I mean), all hot and sweaty. Terry said he had a very round, very smiley face, and that he laughed just like a bear would laugh, a sort of deep bellow of a laugh – when he'd got over the surprise that is. Terry described him as looking like 'a giant pixie in a bearskin'.

For ever afterwards I always held it against Terry that he never took me with him that day down to the dressing-room to meet my polar bear father. I was so envious. Terry had a memory of him now, a real memory. And I didn't. All I had were a few words and a signature on a theatre programme from someone I'd never even met, someone who to me was part polar bear, part actor, part pixie – not at all easy to picture in my head as I grew up.

Picture another Christmas Eve fourteen years later. Upstairs, still at the bottom of my cupboard, my polar bear father in the magazine in the Start-Rite shoebox; and with him all our accumulated childhood treasures:

the signed programme, a battered champion conker (a sixty-fiver!), six silver ball-bearings, four greenish silver threepenny bits (Christmas pudding treasure trove), a Red Devil throat pastille tin with three of my milk teeth cushioned in yellowy cotton wool, and my collection of twenty-seven cowrie shells gleaned over many summers from the beach on Samson in the Scilly Isles. Downstairs, the whole family were gathered in the sitting-room: my mother, Douglas, Terry and my two sisters (half-sisters really, but of course no one ever called them that), Aunty Betty, now married, with twin daughters, my cousins, who were truly awful – I promise you. We were decorating the tree, or rather the twins were fighting over every single dingly-dangly glitter ball, every strand of tinsel. I was trying to fix up the Christmas tree lights which, of course, wouldn't work – again – whilst Aunty Betty was doing her best to avert a war by bribing the dreadful cousins away from the tree with a Mars bar each. It took a while, but in the end she got both of them up on to her lap, and soon they were stuffing themselves contentedly with Mars bars. Blessed peace.

This was the very first Christmas we had had the television. Given half a chance we'd have had it on all the time. But, wisely enough I suppose, Douglas had rationed us to just one programme a day over Christmas. He didn't want the Christmas celebrations interfered with by 'that thing in the corner', as he called it. By common consent, we had chosen the Christmas Eve film on the BBC at five o'clock.

Five o'clock was a very long time coming that day, and when at last Douglas got up and turned on the television, it seemed to take for ever to warm up. Then, there it was on the screen: *Great Expectations* by Charles Dickens. The half-mended lights were at once discarded, the decorating abandoned, as we all settled down to watch in rapt anticipation. Maybe you know the moment: Young Pip is making his way through the graveyard at dusk, mist swirling around him, an owl screeching, gravestones rearing out of the gloom, branches like ghoulish fingers whipping at him as he passes, reaching out to snatch him. He moves through the graveyard timorously, tentatively, like a frightened fawn. Every snap of a twig, every barking fox, every aarking heron sends shivers into our very souls.

Suddenly, a face! A hideous face, a monstrous face, looms up from behind a gravestone. Magwitch, the escaped convict, ancient, craggy and crooked, with long white hair and a straggly beard. A wild man with wild eyes, the eyes of a wolf.

The cousins screamed in unison, long and loud, which broke the tension for all of us and made us laugh. All except my mother.

'Oh my God,' she breathed, grasping my arm. 'That's your father! It is. It's him. It's Peter.'

All the years of pretence, the whole long conspiracy of silence were undone in that one moment. The drama on the television paled into sudden insignificance. The hush in the room was palpable.

Douglas coughed. 'I think I'll fetch some more logs,' he said. And my two half sisters went out with him, in solidarity I think. So did Aunty Betty and the twins; and that left my mother, Terry and me alone together.

I could not take my eyes off the screen. After a while I said to Terry, 'He doesn't look much like a pixie to me.'

'Doesn't look much like a polar bear either,' Terry replied. At Magwitch's every appearance I tried to see through his make-up (I just hoped it *was* make-up!) to discover how my father really looked. It was impossible. My polar bear father, my pixie father had become my convict father.

Until the credits came up at the end my mother never said a word. Then all she said was, 'Well, the potatoes won't peel themselves, and I've got the Brussels sprouts to do as well.' Christmas was a very subdued affair that year, I can tell you.

They say you can't put a genie back in the bottle. Not true. No one in the family ever spoke of the incident afterwards – except Terry and me of course. Everyone behaved as if it had never happened. Enough was enough. Terry and I decided it was time to broach the whole forbidden subject with our mother, in private. We waited until the furore of Christmas was over, and caught her alone in the kitchen one evening. We asked her point blank to tell us about him, our 'first' father, our 'missing' father.

'I don't want to talk about him,' she said. She wouldn't even look at us. 'All I know is that he lives somewhere in Canada now. It was another life. I was another person then. It's not important.' We tried to press her, but that was all she would tell us.

Soon after this I became very busy with my own life, and for some years I thought very little about my convict father, my polar bear father. By the time I was thirty I was married with two sons, and was a teacher trying to become a writer, something I had never dreamt I could be.

Terry had become an actor, something he had always been quite sure he would be. He rang me very late one night in a high state of excitement. 'You'll never guess,' he said. 'He's here! Peter! Our dad. He's here, in England. He's playing in *Henry IV, Part II* in Chichester. I've just read a rave review. He's Falstaff. Why don't we go down there and give him the surprise of his life?'

So we did. The next weekend we went down to Chichester together. I took my family with me. I wanted them to be there for this. He was a wonderful Falstaff, big and boomy, rumbustuous and raunchy, yet full of pathos. My two boys (ten and eight) kept whispering at me every time he came on. 'Is that him? Is that him?' Afterwards we went round to see him in his dressing-room. Terry said I should go in first, and on my own. 'I had my turn a long time ago, if you remember,' he said. 'Best if he sees just one of us to start with, I reckon.'

My heart was in my mouth. I had to take a very deep breath before I knocked on that door. 'Enter.' He sounded still jovial, still Falstaffian. I went in.

He was sitting at his dressing-table in his vest and braces, boots and britches, and humming to himself as he rubbed off his make-up. We looked at each other in the mirror. He stopped humming, and swivelled round to face me. For some moments I just stood there looking at him. Then I said, 'Were you a polar bear once, a long time ago in London?'

'Yes.'

'And were you once the convict in *Great Expectations* on the television?'

'Yes.'

'Then I think I'm your son,' I told him.

There was a lot of hugging in his dressing-room that night, not enough to make up for all those missing years, maybe. But it was a start.

My mother's dead now, bless her heart, but I still have two fathers. I get on well enough with Douglas, I always have done in a detached sort of way. He's done his best by me, I know that: but in all the years I've known him he's never once mentioned my other father. It doesn't matter now. It's history best left crusted over I think.

We see my polar bear father – I still think of him as

that – every year or so, whenever he's over from Canada. He's well past eighty now, still acting for six months of every year – a real trouper. My children and my grandchildren always call him Grandpa Bear because of his great bushy beard (the same one he grew for Falstaff!), and because they all know the story of their grandfather, I suppose.

Recently I wrote a story about a polar bear. I can't imagine why. He's upstairs now reading it to my smallest granddaughter. I can hear him a-snarling and a-growling just as proper polar bears do. Takes him back, I should think. Takes me back, that's for sure.

Other authors in the series

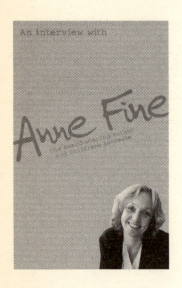

An interview with

Anne Fine

The award-winning author and children's laureate

An interview with

J. K. Rowling

Creator of the best-selling Harry Potter

An interview with

Jamila Gavin

The best-selling author of Coram Boy

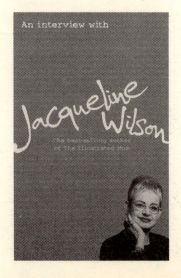

An interview with

Jacqueline Wilson

The best-selling author of The Illustrated Mum